Training Sessions For Soccer Coaches Volume 2

Training Sessions For Soccer Coaches, Volume 2

Chris King

Published by Chris King, 2023.

TRAINING SESSIONS FOR SOCCER COACHES VOLUME 2

First edition. August 31, 2023.

ISBN: 979-8215267516

Written by Chris King.

TRAINING SESSIONS FOR

SOCCER COACHES

VOLUME 2

Coaching Books For Amateur Soccer Coaches

CHRIS KING

KING SOCCER COACH

TRAINING SESSIONS FOR SOCCER COACHES - VOLUME 2

INTRODUCTION

This book is for soccer coaches who want to improve their training sessions. The drills in this book are explained step by step and include diagrams. They will have you running a quality training session in no time! The drills are aimed at all levels of players.

These training sessions have been chosen because they work in real life, not just in a book. I have played and coached for over 30 years and I ran these sessions last season. These drills will bring improvement and better results to you and your team.

These drills are 100% on the ball so they improve endurance, technique, and tactics all at the same time plus you'll see your players enjoying the sessions more.

If you're a new coach, or you're simply a coach that hasn't had the time to work on your sessions, this book will improve you immensely. Game day results start on the training track and if the coach doesn't have a good training session planned, the players won't improve and will lose motivation.

Most drills can be adjusted to suit the number of players you have at your session. I understand that on any night player numbers vary, so most of these drills are adjustable for more or less players.

I've completed coaching courses and coached senior men's teams, ladies, youth and junior teams. The advice and drills in this book will get you up and running straight away. Don't jump on YouTube an hour before training looking for a fancy drill - simply choose a session from this book, follow the step by step guides and you will see your sessions and coaching ability improve straight away (plus you'll enjoy coaching more!).

"Training Sessions for Soccer Coaches - Volume 2" lays out full training sessions that will improve different parts of your team's game. It walks you through what to do from the warm up to the warm down and all the drills in between.

The drills focus on one main aspect per session and you are given three different drills per session that build on each other. In this, my second soccer coaching book, you will learn how to run sessions for these four key components of the game:

1. **Playing Out From The Back**

2. **Pressing**
3. **Midfield Play**
4. **Supporting The Attack**

Also in this book you'll also find general advice on things that help your session run smoother which will give you confidence as a coach. Some of it might not seem important, but over a season they will save you time and you will become more organised.

The **drills are all aimed at improving players technical ability** and all of the drills are 'on the ball'. I believe in getting fit and improving skill through football based drills, not just running for the sake of running. As a coach, you may only have the players for two 90 minutes sessions a week, so the training sessions laid out in this book help you get maximum value out of those sessions.

Before you jump into the first session, please spend 5 minutes reading the following chapter which breaks down how a general training session should be structured.

Happy Coaching!

Chris King

Online Kids Coaching Course on Udemy.com:

https://www.udemy.com/course/

howtocoachkidssoccer/?referralCode=CCFEDDB18FE0AAF8F1CC

And if you need other coaching books have a look below. I have full coaching sessions for senior players down to coaching kids soccer for parents or volunteers. Just search for:

"Chris King Soccer Coach" or follow the links below:

www.chriskingsoccercoach.com[1]

VIEW OTHER SOCCER COACHING BOOKS BY CHRIS KING

Training Sessions For Soccer Coaches Volume 1

Training Sessions For Soccer Coaches Volume 2

Training Sessions For Soccer Coaches Volume 3

1. http://www.chriskingsoccercoach.com

Attacking & Shooting Drills For Soccer Coaches

Soccer Rondos Volume 1

Soccer Rondos Volume 2

Coaching Kids Soccer - Volume 1

Coaching Kids Soccer - Volume 2

Coaching Kids Soccer - Volume 3

TRAINING SESSION STRUCTURE

A training session should run for approximately 90 minutes (not including initial warm up or warm down). Let's break it down into an average Tuesday night training session at my club. Listed below is how I run my session so you can see...

6:00-6:10: Players on the pitch (Light Warm Up)

6:10-6:15: Training Starts: Coach talk

6:15-6:35: Warm up (the FIFA 11+)

6:35-6:55: Drill 1 (Rondo)

7:00-7:20: Drill 2 (Positioning Game)

7:20-7:40: Drill 3 (Game Training)

7:40-8:05: Game (Match Practice)

8:05-8:10: Warm Down

As you can see, the session is broken down into 8 parts. You will only be heavily involved in taking 3 parts (Drills 1,2,3) because the 'Warm up', 'Warm down' and 'Game' all stay the same. Drills 1,2 and 3 are the drills that change and work on parts of your team's game and are all covered in this book.

1. PLAYERS ON THE PITCH: They should be changed, ready and doing individual light warm ups (foam roller, band stretching, etc).

2. TRAINING STARTS: COACH TALK: A short 5 minute talk by the coach (you!) on the areas that will be covered in tonight's session (this helps you get player 'buy in' for the session. Players start to understand they're here to learn and work hard alongside having fun).

3. WARM UP: The Warm Up should be the FIFA 11+ every time (and most parts of this should be performed before a match as well). It has been proven to reduce injuries and players bond at the same time.

4. DRILL 1 (RONDO): Next is always Drill 1 which is referred to as a Rondo (a simple short, sharp drill that gets the players body and mind warmed up for the session). This runs for approximately 15-20 minutes.

5. DRILL 2 (POSITIONING GAME): Drill 2 is referred to as a Positioning Game. It is used to get the players thinking about where they are (or should be) on the pitch. The drill is in a small area so they get lots of chances to repeat the parts that are being worked on. This should run for approximately 20 minutes.

6. DRILL 3 (GAME TRAINING): Drill 3 is referred to as Game Training. It is usually an expanded version of Drill 2 but in a larger and more match realistic situation. This should run for appropriately 20 minutes.

7. GAME: It does what it says on the tin - it's time for a game (11v11, 5v5, whatever your numbers are). At the end of the night you should always have a Game, it's great to do drills but eventually it's got to be implemented in a match situation, so this is when you do it. There shouldn't be many (if any) restrictions. Let your players play and hopefully they implement what you have been working on in the session. Look for key moments from the session that night that you have been working on that appear during the game. Then stop the game briefly to point out what they are doing right or incorrectly. But generally just let the game flow and observe your players.

8. WARM DOWN: The warm down should be 10 minutes of light jogging, walking and intermittent static stretching.

So that's a general overview of what a training session should look like.

That's enough for now, I'm sure you want to start looking through the first drills, so read on and use my session plans and watch your coaching improve!

P.S. There's an index at the back of the book for a few terms that will pop up that you may not be familiar with. Plus the FIFA 11+ Warm Up is covered towards the end of the book.

P.P.S. In most of the larger drills when there are large numbers of players, the players number represents their position on the field. Here is the number alongside the players position and how they would line up in a typical 4-3-3 formation. This numbering system helps to give you an idea of what type of player should be in that position. So if you see a number 6 in a larger drill, you'll know it should be a holding midfielder in that position.

1 - Goalkeeper

2 - Right Full Back

3 - Centre Back

4 - Centre Back

5 - Left Full Back

6 - Holding Midfielder

7 - Right Wing

8 - Forward Midfielder

9 - Striker

10 - Forward Midfielder

11 - Left Wing

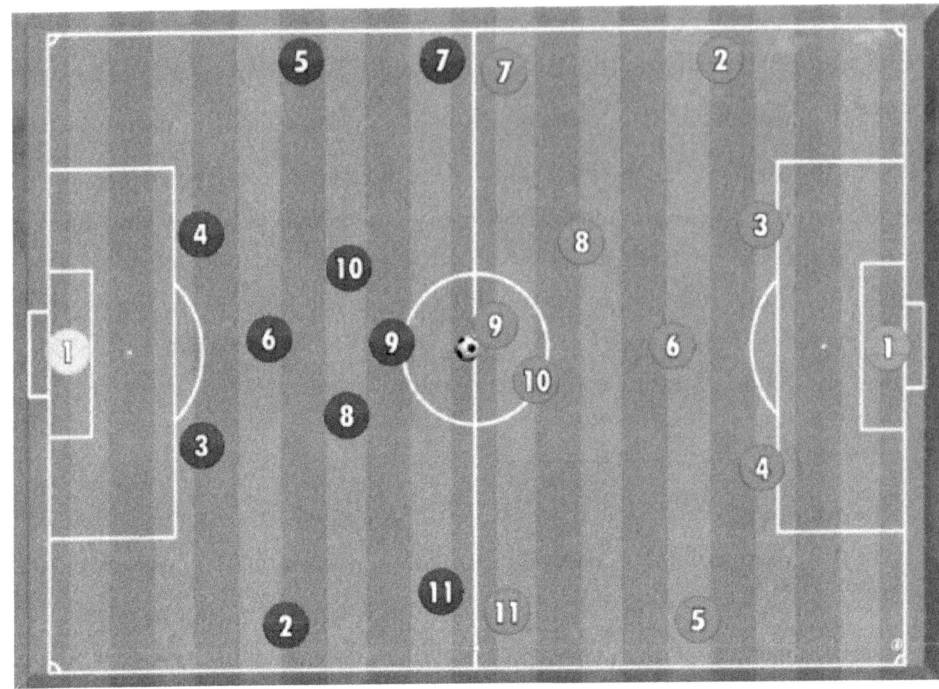
5
7
7
2
4
10
8
3
6
9
9
6
1
10
1
8
3
4
11
11
2
5

SESSION 1 - TRANSITION FROM DEFENCE TO ATTACK

Parts of the players game that will be improved from this session:

Conditioning (fitness); Transitioning.

Players will become aware of how important it is to quickly move from defence to attack so as to catch the opposition when they are out of their defensive shape.

SESSION 1 DRILL 1:

RONDO: GOING FROM DEFENCE TO ATTACK

PURPOSE:

To improve fitness, pressing and transitioning from defence to attack.

SET UP:

- 8 Players (alternatively 6,7, 9 or 10 players. With 6 or 10 players make it 3v1 or 5v2. With 7 and 9 make it 3v1 with an overload player who plays with the team in possession or 4v2 with an overload. Adjust area accordingly)
- 4 Cones + 3 Discs
- 30x30 yard area
- 15 Minutes

THE DRILL:

Two teams of 4, with a 4v2 in one half and the other 2 team mates resting in the other half.

When the 2 defensive players win the ball they quickly transition to the other half and play 'keep offs' with 2 players from the team that just lost the ball quickly moving to the other half and trying to win the ball back.

KEY POINTS:

- Focus on the 2 defensive players pressing the ball carrier to win it back early on before the team in possession gets settled.

COACHES NOTES:

- Run the drill for 2-3 minutes and then rest the players for 1 minute. Go through 3 times. This will work on their fitness and ability to work and press when fatigued. This is a good pre-season drill to work on conditioning.

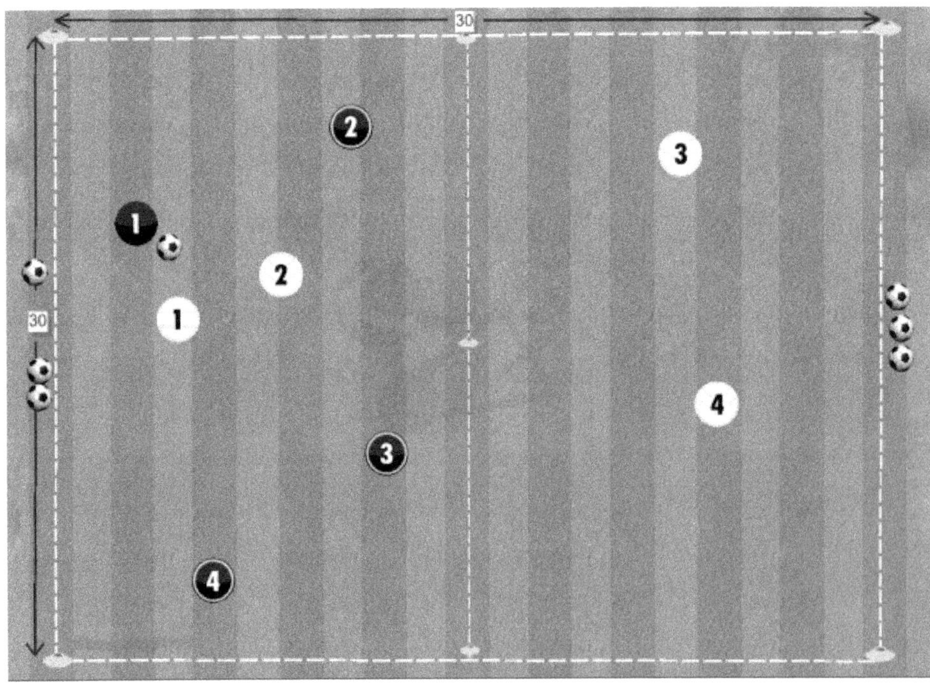

Starting shape: *4v2 with two resting. Blacks start in possession and pass between themselves playing keep offs. As soon as White wins it they transition to the other half and two Blacks follow to try and win it back. Work for 2-3 minutes with 1 minute rest in between. Go through 3-4 times.*

Notice how the two Whites are pressing together and trying to get Black to pass to the area they want so they have a better chance of winning it in a contained area.

(Image: Session 1 Drill 1 - A)

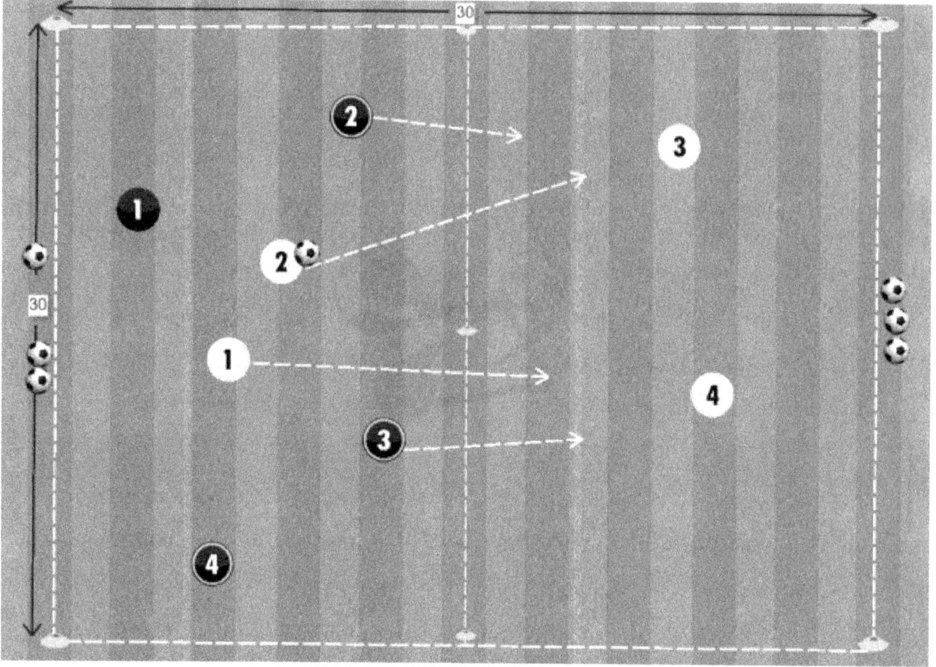

In play: Once White #2 has won the ball, he passes (or dribbles) as quickly as possible to his half. His team mate follows and two players from the Black team transition across to try and win the ball (they should try and win it back before the Whites get to their half if possible).

This should be a high intensity and non stop drill.

(Image: Session 1 Drill 1 - B)

SESSION 1 DRILL 2:

TRANSITIONING WITH COMBINATIONS TO ATTACK

PURPOSE:

Focus the attackers (Black) on quick, short combinations to pass their way to their #9.

Focus the defenders (in this case Whites) on a quick transition into attack when they win the ball. Get them in the habit of playing forward as quickly as possible to catch the opposition out of shape.

SET UP:

- 9 Players (alternatively 7,8, 10 or 11. With 7 or 8 use the coach as the Grey or use a small goal instead of the striker [Black #9] at the end. For 11 or 12 simply add 1 or 2 more Blacks on the outside wings).
- 4 Cones
- 20x15 yard area
- 20 minutes

THE DRILL:

6v3. There are 6 attackers (5xBlacks and 1xGrey) v 2 defenders (3xWhites) aiming to get it through to their striker (Black #9). Continuous play from one end to the other.

All outside players can move anywhere along their line. The other 5 players in the middle must stay in the middle.

Play starts with the Grey player (acting as a centre back or goalkeeper) from the end line and is played into a Black. Whites must try to stop Blacks getting from the Grey to the Black #9 (or visa versa).

Blacks #2 & #3 cannot play it directly to Black #9, it must go through a Black player in the middle (#8 or #10) who can pass to Black #9.

If Whites win possession they are to play it as quickly as possible to the Grey player (they cannot use the outside Black players).

If they can get it to the Grey player in 3 passes or under they are awarded 2 goals, if it's over 3 passes they are awarded 1 goal. This is to encourage a fast transition and ball movement.

Blacks are awarded 1 goal when they get it to their striker (Black #9) or Grey #5.

KEY POINTS:

- Speed of transition when the ball is won by Whites.

COACHES NOTES:

- Can the players find space in this tight area?
- Can the players beat their opponent if there is not an obvious option?
- Black #8 & #10 should be 'head checking' to see their options.

CHANGES:

Punish Whites (take a goal off) if they do not get it to the Grey player when they win the ball (it is 3v2 in Whites favour in the middle so the should be able to transition the ball quickly and effectively)

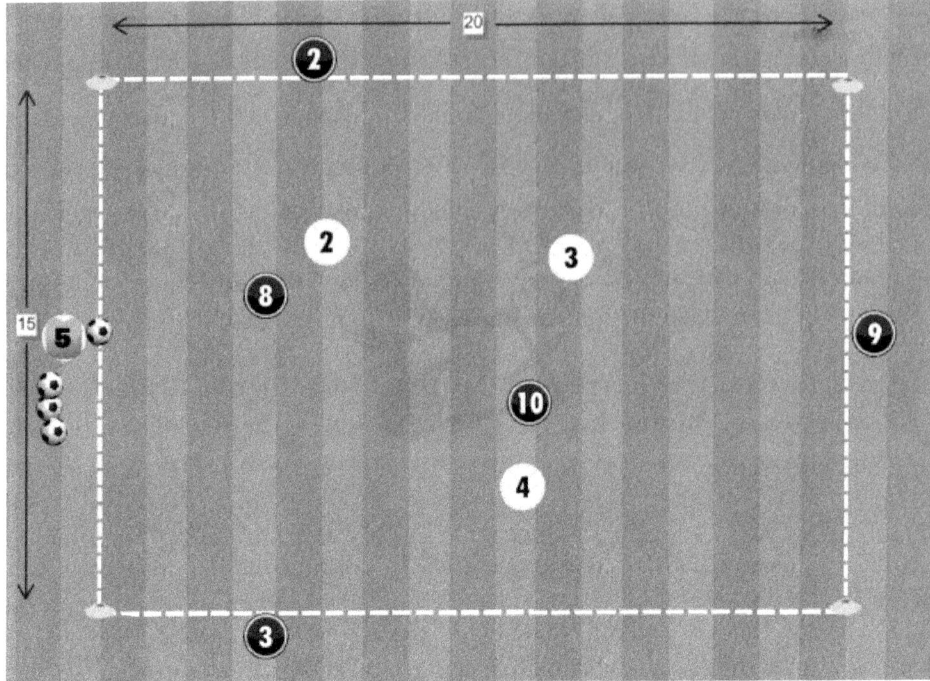

Starting shape: Grey #5 starts play and passes into a central Black. From here the Blacks can re-use the Grey #5 or outside Blacks (#2 & #3) who can move in support up and down the outside lines. The final pass to Black #9 must come from a central Black player.

If White wins possession, they are to move the ball as quickly as possible (a quick transition) and pass the ball to the Grey player in the least amount of passes possible.

(Image: Session 1 Drill 2 - A)

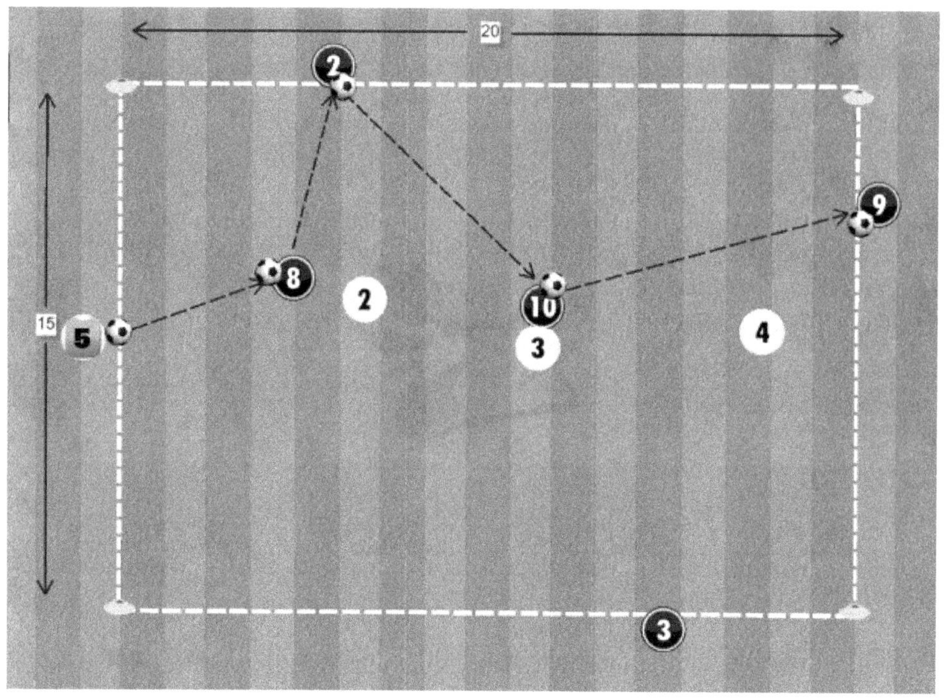

In play: Grey passes to Black #8 who uses Black #2. The ball must now come back into the central area (Black #10) before they can pass to their striker (Black #9). Play then continues working back the other way to Grey #5. Remember, When Whites win possession their aim is to get it to Grey #5 as quickly as possible! This helps teach them the importance of speed of transition.

(Image: Session 1 Drill 2 - B)

SESSION 1 DRILL 3:

COUNTER ATTACKING GAME

PURPOSE:

Getting the players used to instantly thinking counter attack when they win possession as the opposition will be out of defensive formation.

SET UP:

- 18 Players including 2 Goalkeepers (Alternatively 12 to 22 players. Add or remove players as needed and adjust the size of the area accordingly)

- 4 Cones

- 2 x large goals (small or medium if no large)

- 80x50 yard area

- 20 minutes

THE DRILL:

9v9 (including 2x goalkeepers). A medium sided game with the offside rule applying.

3-4-1 formation.

Teams are looking for a quick transition from defence to attack when they win the ball and looking to get support in numbers.

KEY POINTS:

- Quick transition (from defence into attack and visa versa).

- Support the attack in numbers.

COACHES NOTES:

- Get the players to have lots of shots on goals. If a team scores they keep the ball and play restarts from their goalkeeper.

- Encourage players to get forward in numbers when they have possession.

If you need more attacking drills Chris Kings book has a variety of drills for all levels of players in "Attacking & Shooting Drills For Soccer Coaches"

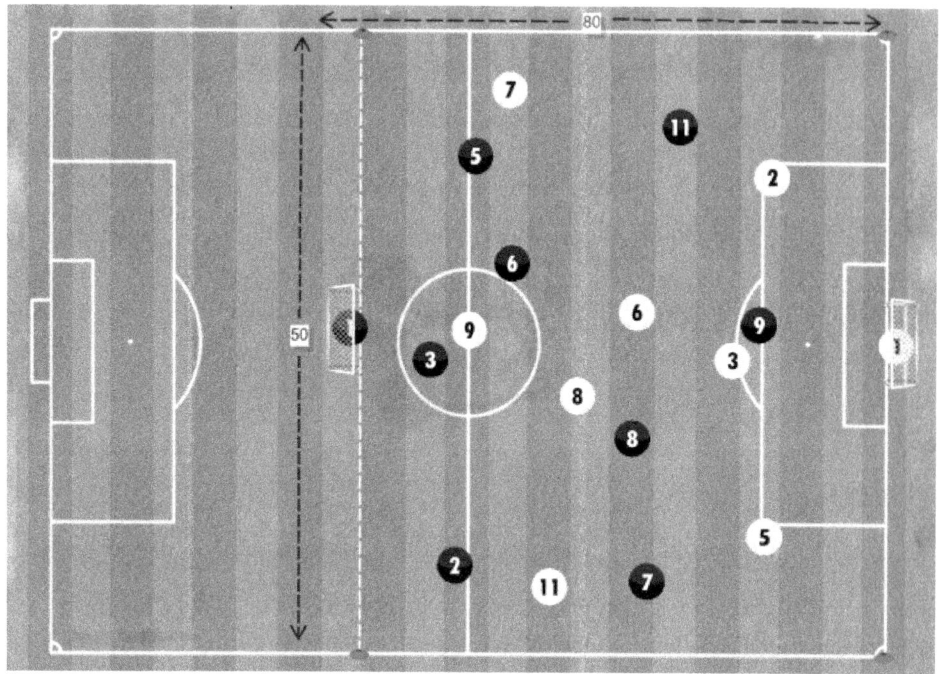

Starting shape: Ideally play with a back 3 (#2,#3,#5), 2 midfielders (#6,#8), 2 wingers (#7,#11) and 1 striker (#9). Look for high intensity and quick movement from defence into attack and from attack into the defensive shape. (Image: Session 1 Drill 3 - A)

SESSION 2 - MIDFIELD DIAMOND SHAPE

The players will gain awareness on what shape the midfield should have when in attack and when in defence.

SESSION 2 DRILL 1:

2v2+2 RONDO

PURPOSE:

To get the players used to providing options to the player on the ball by getting in a diamond shape. This shape helps present an option to the left, right, short and higher up.

SET UP:

- 6 Players (Alternatively 7,8 or 9. For 7 and 8 players add in an overload of players that always play with the team in possession. For 9, add a player to each team so it's 3+3v3. Adjust the size of the area accordingly)
- 4 Cones
- 20x20 yard area
- 15 minutes

THE DRILL:

- 2+2v2 in a 20x20 yard area. 2 players in Black bibs, 2 players in White bibs, 2 players in Grey bibs.
- 4 players (ie 2xBlacks plus 2x Whites) keep possession v the 2xGrey.

- The two teams keep possession for as long as possible. Once the Grey team wins possession (or the ball goes out of the area) they work alongside the other team. The team that gave away possession become the defenders.

KEY POINTS:

- Quick, continuous play.
- Lots of talk and organising.

COACHES NOTES:

- Focus on the shape of the team in possession. When they have good possession there should be three good options for the player on the ball - she should have a teammate on her left, right and one higher up. This spreads the defenders and creates good options.
-
- Have lots of balls spread around the area so play is continuous.

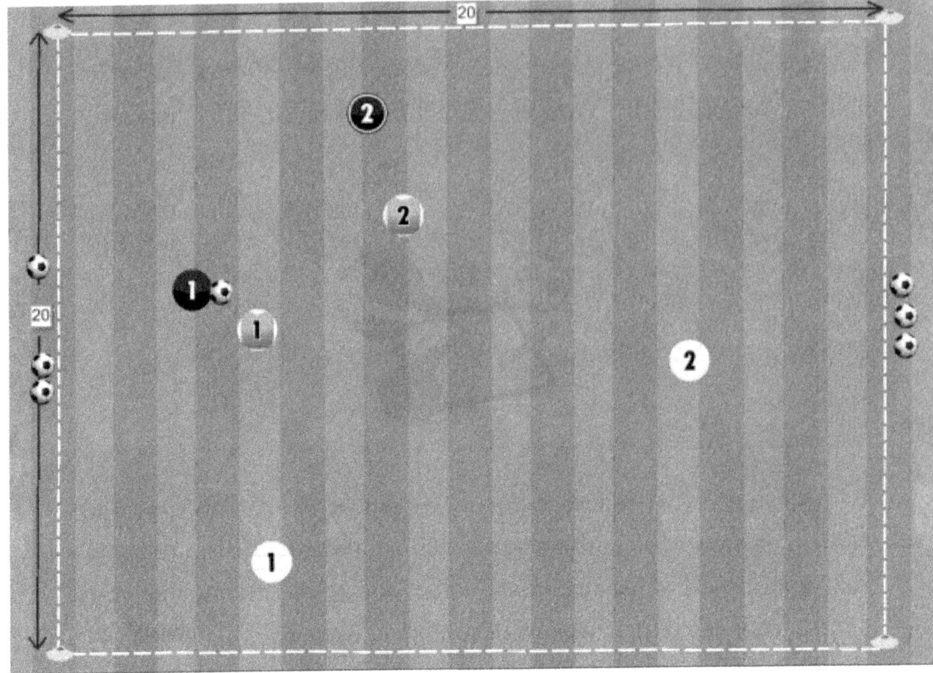

Starting shape: 2 Blacks + 2 Whites work together to keep possession off the 2 Greys. Notice how their shape is a diamond so it provides options for the ball carrier left, right and high. Once the 2 Grey players win the ball or the ball goes out of the area off an attacking player they work with the other team and the team that lost possession becomes the defenders.

Also notice how the Grey #1 is pressing the ball carrier on the side where she doesn't want them to play out of. She wants the Black #1 to pass to Black #2 as that is the side that her teammate Grey #2 has moved to.

(Image: Session 2 Drill 1 - A)

SESSION 2 DRILL 2:

DEFENCE TO ATTACK THROUGH A GOOD MIDFIELD SHAPE

PURPOSE:

To get the ball from the backline to the striker using the diamond midfield.

SET UP:

- 9 Players (Alternatively 8, 10, or 11. For 8 use the coach as the #3 to play balls in. For 10 and 11 players add in a defender against the Black #9 and add in a White defender to make it 4v4 in the midfield).
- 8 Cones + 2 Discs
- 30x40 yard area
- 20 minutes

THE DRILL:

The play starts from Black #3.

Blacks try to move it through the midfield, to the striker (Black #9) who plays it back ('bounces') to the Black Midfield who can then score in the small goals. (Note: Black can also play it back to Black #3 at any time).

If White intercept they can score in the small goals behind Black #3 - they must score with in 10 seconds otherwise play is stopped and restarts from Black #3.

KEY POINTS:

- Make sure to have a good midfield shape.
- Get players forward to support and use the bounce pass off the striker (Black #9).

COACHES NOTES:

- Get the players to keep the diamond shape, so as one midfield comes deep to receive the ball - another one stay high and the other two are left and right

- The middle four can rotate and change positions but must keep their shape

- When the Blacks lose possession, Blacks #6 & #8 drop in to block the passing lanes (in this case the passing lanes are to the goals so they should be blocking the goal that is on the side where the ball is).

PROGRESSION:

- Add a defensive player into the attacking zone

- Add one more defensive midfield player

- Restrict players to 2 touch only

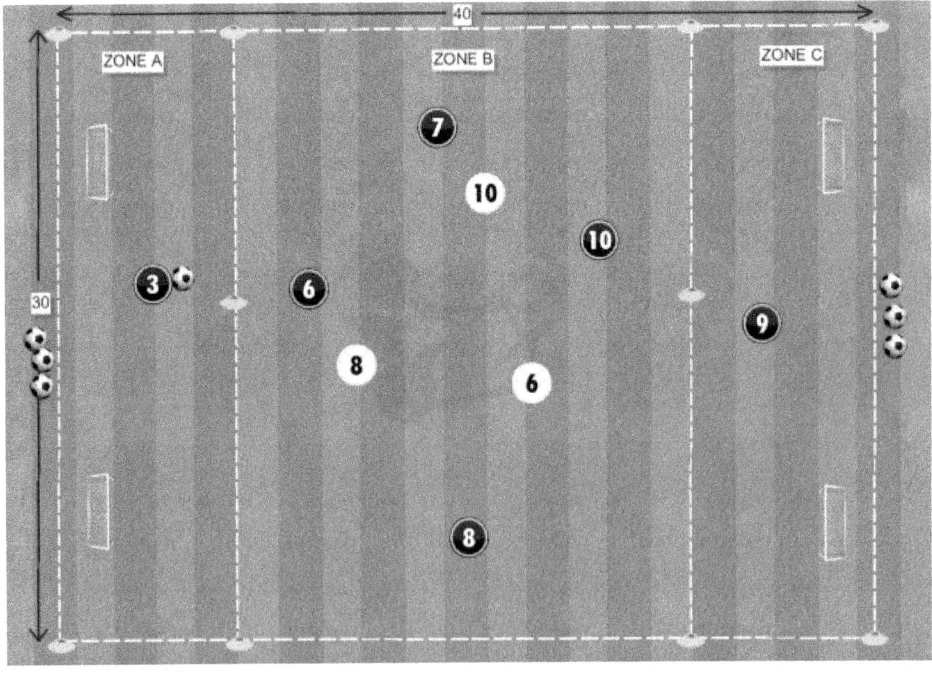

Starting shape: Black #3 plays it into a Black midfielder. Notice their diamond shape to provide options left, right, near and high (same as the Rondo in drill 1). If White win possession they must score in the small goals behind Black #3 within 10 seconds.

(Image: Session 2 Drill 2 - A)

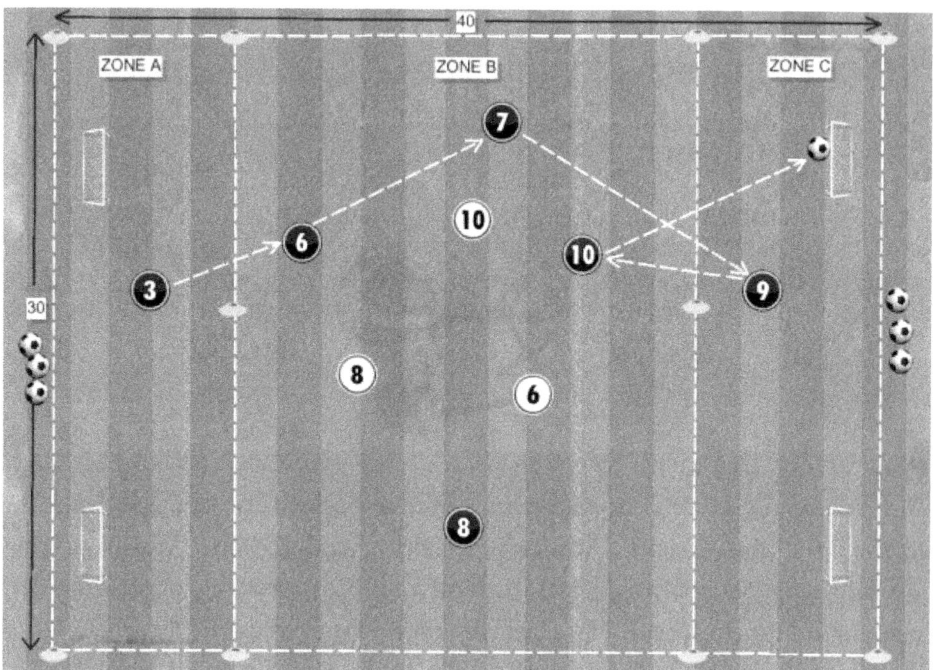

In Play: Black have played it up to Black #9 who plays it back into Black #10 who finishes in the small goal. Play then restarts from Black #3.

(Image: Session 2 Drill 2 - B)

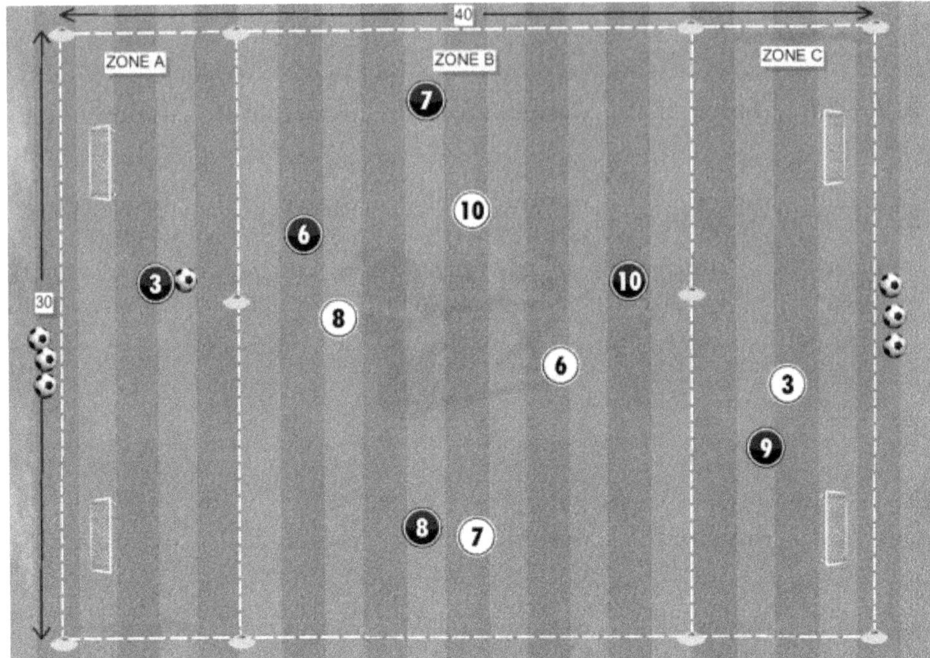

Progression: This is with 11 players (please note: you could add another defend and attacker in Zone C as well because the main focus of this drill is on the midfield 4 shape) - It is now 4v4 in the midfield and the Black striker #9 now has a White defender to contend with, making it a more realistic game situation. It is a maximum of 2 touches for all players so the ball is moved quickly.

(Image: Session 2 Drill 2 - C)

SESSION 2 DRILL 3:

MIDFIELD DIAMOND SHAPE

PURPOSE:

To get good midfield shape which provides options when in possession and blocks passing lanes when not in possession.

SET UP:

- 18 Players (Alternatively 16 or 14 - remove the wingers and/or goalkeepers)
- 12 Cones + 4 Discs
- 40x50 yard area
- 2 Large goal (or 1 large goal and poles for the other one or 2 small goals)
- 20 minutes

THE DRILL:

There are 3 Zones: 2v1 in Zones A & C. 4v4 in Zone B.

1 attacker v 2 defenders in Zones A & C.

There are 2 wing backs on the outside of Zone B who play on the team in possession.

The team in possession may bring in an extra player to the next Zone as they move forward, creating an overload.

Shoots must be taken from inside Zone A & C (players cannot encroach into the goalkeepers area). If a team scores they keep possession and play restarts from their goalkeeper.

KEY POINTS:

- Both teams keep a good midfield shape. The team in possession in a diamond shape, the opposition deepest 2 midfielders drop off to block passing lanes.

COACHES NOTES:

- Make sure to keep the midfield shape as a diamond as per the previous drills. You always want an option left, right and high.

- Midfielders can rotate positions to make them hard to mark but make sure to keep the diamond shape.

PROGRESSION:

1 wingback can enter Zone A or C of the team in possession (they can support the attack)

Remove all the Zones and let them play freely, still using the wing backs as players on the team in possession.

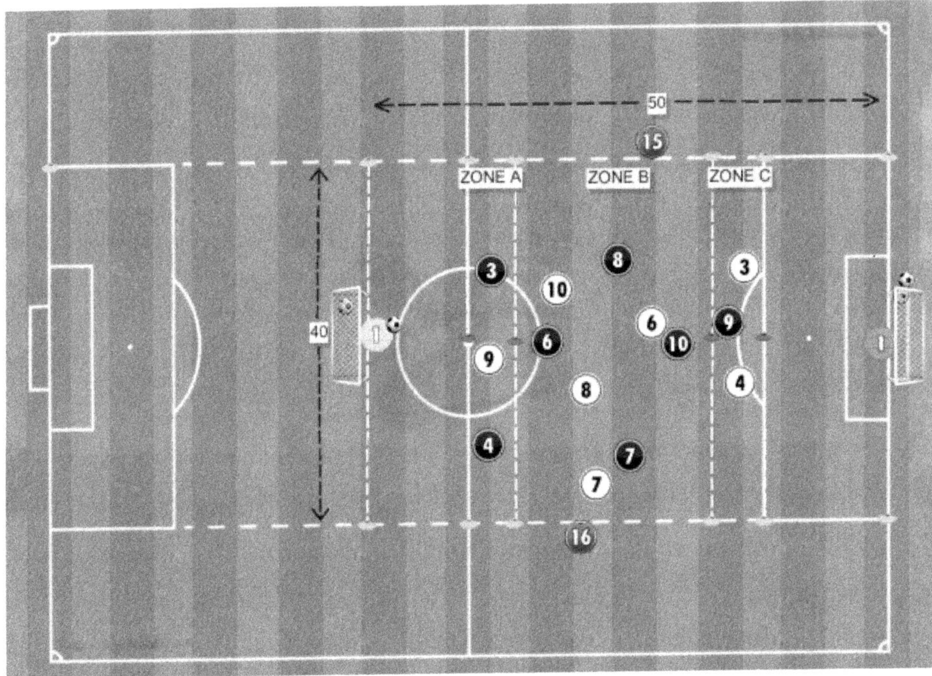

Starting shape: 1 attacker v 2 defenders in Zones A & C. 4v4 in Zone B. 2 wing backs play on the team in possession. The team in possession have a good diamond midfield shape (in this case Black) with the opposition midfield pressing and blocking passing lanes. Midfielders from both sides should be 'head checking' so see where they can pass or where their opposite number is so they can block off the passing lane to them.

(Image: Session 2 Drill 3 - A)

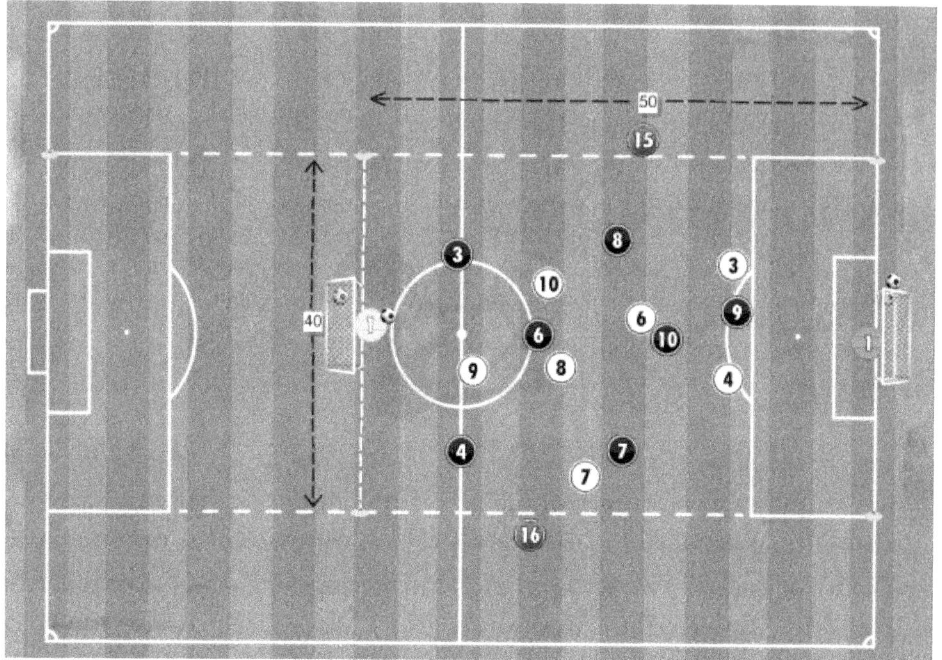

Progression: With the Zones removed play should still be structured. The wingbacks continue to play on the team in possession.

(Image: Session 2 Drill 3 - B)

SESSION 3 - DEFENSIVE RESTING POSITIONS

(TO HELP THE PRESS)

The team will gain awareness on what shape the players not directly involved in the play should be in to help the press and stop the ball getting out.

SESSION 3 DRILL 1:

4v2 RONDO

PURPOSE:

To get the defensive players to work together so as not to get split by the pass. If they can stop this splitting pass and make the attacking team go sideways they have done their job. It will allow defensive players further up the field to join in and help win the ball. This drill also works on the attacking player's first touch to take the ball away from the defender.

SET UP:

- 6 Players (Alternatively 7 or 8. For 7 players make it 5v2 and for 8 players make it 5v3. Adjust the size of the area accordingly)
- 4 Cones
- 20x20 yard area
- 15 minutes

THE DRILL:

4v2 in a 20x20 yard area. 4 Black players around the outside, 2 White players as defenders in the middle. Outside players (Black) cannot enter the area. The 2 Defenders (White) can tackle the outside players.

4 Black players move the ball quickly between themselves. The 2 defenders look to win the ball. Once a defender wins the ball, the outside player quickly swaps with them.

KEY POINTS:

- Quick, continuous play.
- Lots of talk and organising, especially between the 2 defenders.
- 2 defenders work together to block the pass and corner the attacker.
- Outside players look to split the 2 defenders with the pass when possible.
- Outside players should look to take 2 touches where possible - the first one taking it away from the defender so they can make a good pass without the defender being right on them.

COACHES NOTES:

- Focus on the shape of the 2 defenders. Are they working together and pressing the ball carrier? Are they talking to each other to say where they are and motivating each other?
- Tell the defenders to not get split by the pass. Their job is to either win the ball or hold up the attackers.
- Have lots of balls spread around the area so play is continuous.

PROGRESSION:

After the players have been going for 5 minutes (swapping each time they win the ball with the player who made the mistake) change it up. Now get the players in the middle to work in pairs for 2 minutes at a time. If they get split it's 2 push ups each time at the end of the two minutes. And if the attackers put together 10 passes it's also 2 push ups to the defenders at the end. This will help both sides keep the intensity up.

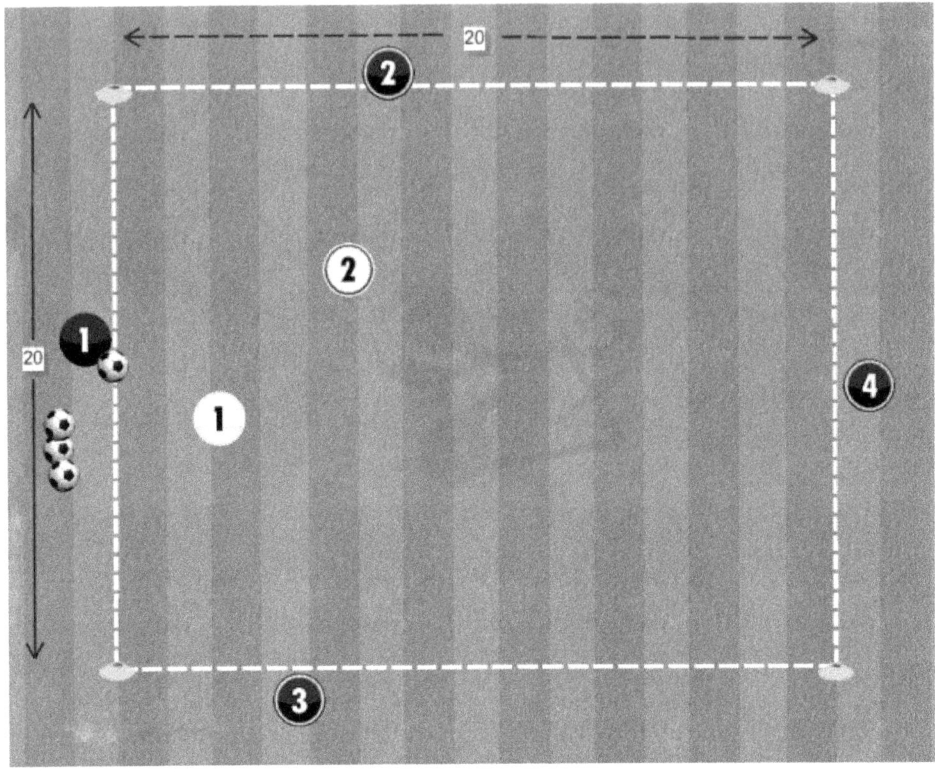

Starting shape: Players around the outside are free to move along their lines. They are looking to pass the ball around quickly until an opportunity arises to split the defenders. The two Whites work together, pressing the player in possession.

Here the White #1 is pressing Black #1 and blocking off the pass to Black #3 which will allow White #2 to possibly win the ball if Black #1's only option is to pass to Black #2.

(Image: Session 3 Drill 1 - A)

SESSION 3 DRILL 2:

DEFENSIVE PLAYERS SET UP

PURPOSE:

To get players to set up in good defensive positions when their team loses the ball, with their aim to keep the ball high up the field and allow their teammates to win back possession.

SET UP:

- 10 to 20 Players (split the group into two separate groups. For example, if you have 20 players split into 2 lots of 10 players and then it will be 5v5 in each group).
- 6 Cones + 3 Discs
- 30x40 yard area
- 20 minutes

THE DRILL:

5v5 with Blacks starting in possession.

As soon as the first pass is made, 2 Whites can enter the other half to try and win possession.

Once Whites win possession they try to pass or dribble back to the other half to their teammates.

At the same time, as soon as Blacks lose possession, the two deepest players should set up across the halfway line to block the easy pass out for the White team back to their teammates.

Play is continuous, with players from the defensive team rotating who goes across each time.

KEY POINTS:

- Make sure that the team in possession has a good shape. They should spread out around the square.

- Get the player on the team in possession to move the ball to the side of their body where the defender isn't (as they should have been doing in the Rondo earlier). This creates good habits and keeps good possession.

- When a team wins possession they should look to transition back to their half quickly before the opposition has time to block the passing lanes.

COACHES NOTES:

- Get the players to work hard continuously. Stop every 5 minutes for a quick recovery and work on tasks with them (ie are attackers moving the ball away from the defender with their first touch? Are defenders transitioning quickly back to their half when they win possession? And most importantly, are the deepest players from the team that just lost possession setting up to block the passing lanes straight away?)

- Make sure the attacking team is spread out around the square.

- Make sure the two defenders that are getting across to win the ball get across quickly. The best time to win possession back is before a team can get in shape and get organised.

- Both sides should be doing lots of talking and organising to make sure their shape is right and players are pushing over to the other half straight away.

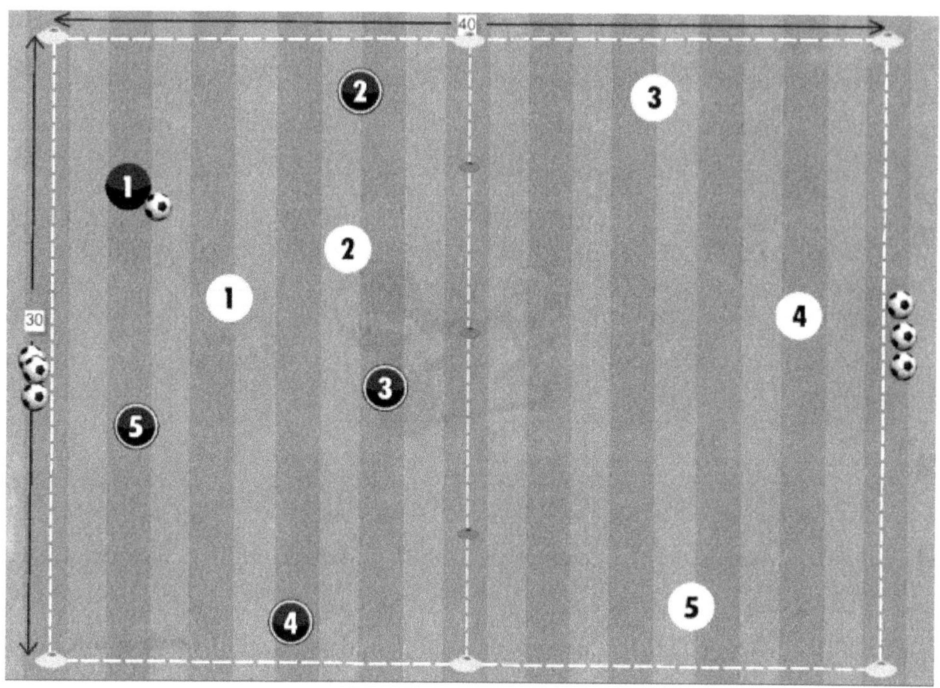

Starting shape: In this 5v5 the Black team have spread out to provide options for the ball carrier and to make it harder for the defenders to block passing lanes.

(Image: Session 3 Drill 2- A)

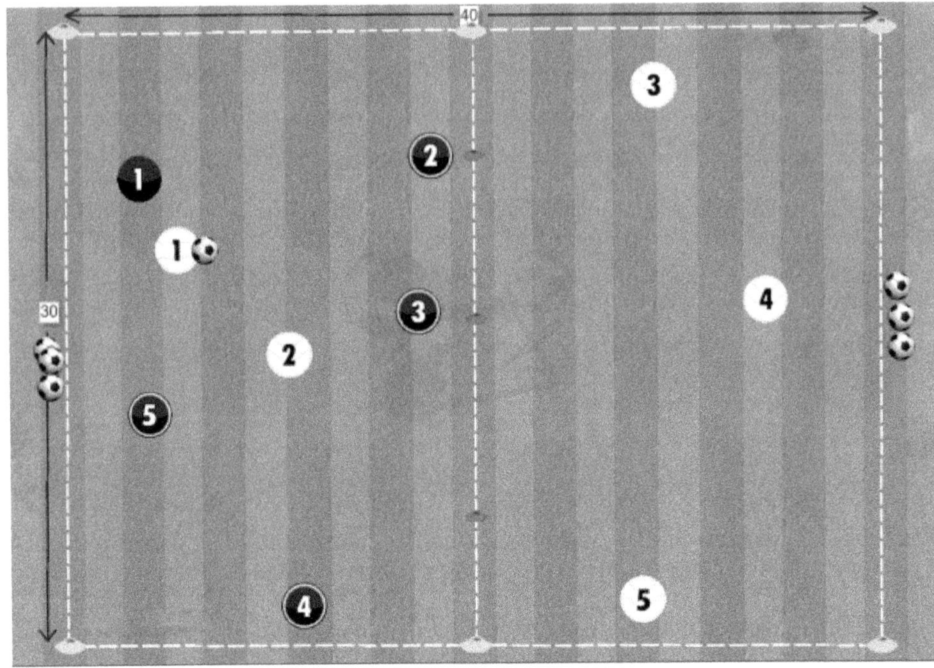

In play - 1: Here the two Whites have just won possession. The two deepest Black players drop into the dangerous area which is the area on the side that the ball is. Note that their positioning is blocking the passing lanes to White #3 & White #4. This stops the easy out and will keep the ball in their half for that vital extra second that may allow Blacks to win the ball back.

(Image: Session 3 Drill 2 - B)

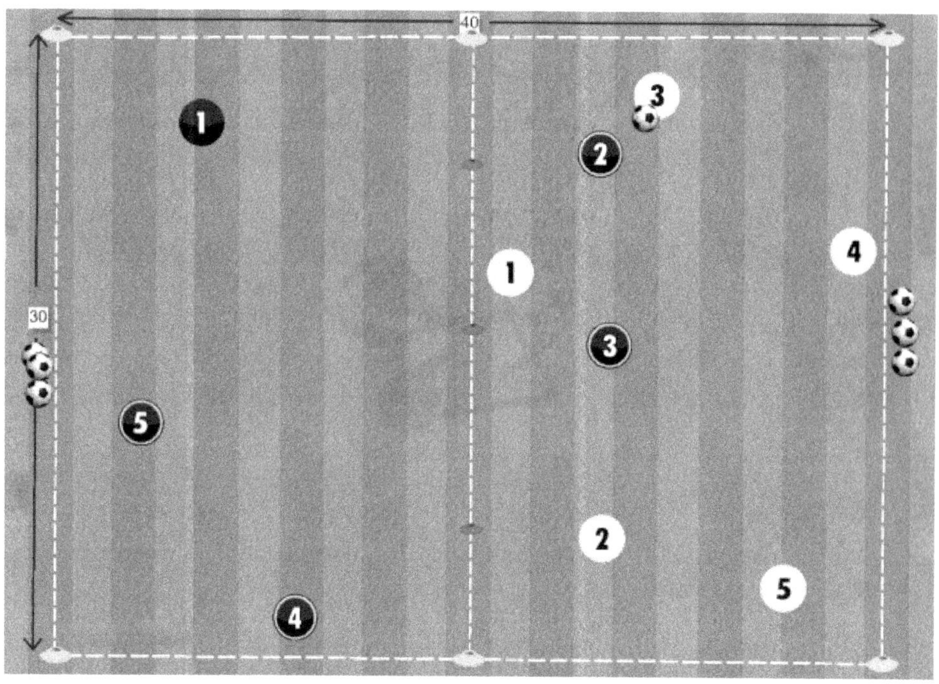

In play - 2 : Whites have transitioned across quickly and two Blacks have followed to try and win it back before they're settled which is what we want to achieve.

(Image: Session 3 Drill 2 - C)

SESSION 3 DRILL 3: HALF PITCH HIGH INTENSITY GAME

PURPOSE:

Working as a team and organising each other to make sure players do their jobs.

SET UP:

- 20 Players including 2 GK (Alternatively 12 to 21. Adjust the size of the area accordingly)
- 4 Cones
- 40x50 yard area
- 2 Large goals (or 1 large goal and poles for the other one. Or if no Goalkeepers just use small goals)
- 20 minutes

THE DRILL:

3 teams of 6 players - 2 teams on, with the third team resting on the side. If you only have enough for 2 teams that's also perfect.

Formations for each team should be as follows:

5 players: 2-2-1

6 players: 2-3-1

7 players: 3-3-1

As soon as a goal is scored the team that was scored on goes off and the resting team comes on. Play starts from the team that just scored. This makes the team coming on get on and organised quickly.

KEY POINTS:

• Get the highest midfielder to support the attack and get a full back to push on where possible. You want to have as many forwards with an attack as possible.

• Players on the defensive team not directly involved in the play should be looking at blocking the passing lanes and pushing to the side where the ball is (adjusting their positions as the ball moves).

• If you only have 2 teams, have a 45 second rest every 5 minutes. This will give the players a chance to reset and keep the intensity up and will give you a chance to highlight what is working and what needs to be adjusted.

COACHES NOTES:

• When a team wins possession, get them to move the ball forward as quickly as possible to catch the opposition out of position. And on the flip side, get the team that has just lost possession to get back in their defensive shape and to block the passing lanes straight away.

• If the game is going too long without a goal being scored, give the two teams a 20 second warning and then take off the team that has been on the longest. This stops the resting team being off for too long and also keeps the intensity up on the pitch.

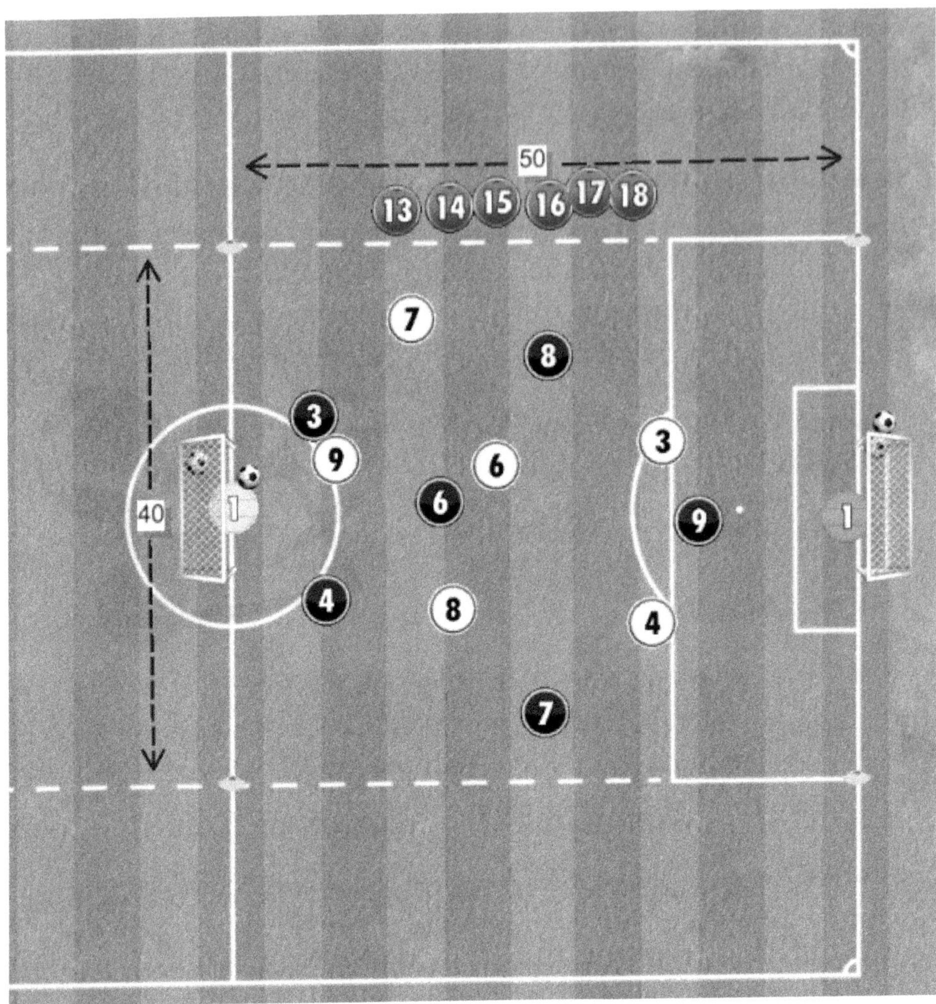

Starting shape: If there are 6 players on each side the formation should be 2-3-1 as seen below. The resting team should be ready to go as soon as there is a goal scored.

(Image: Session 3 Drill 3 - A)

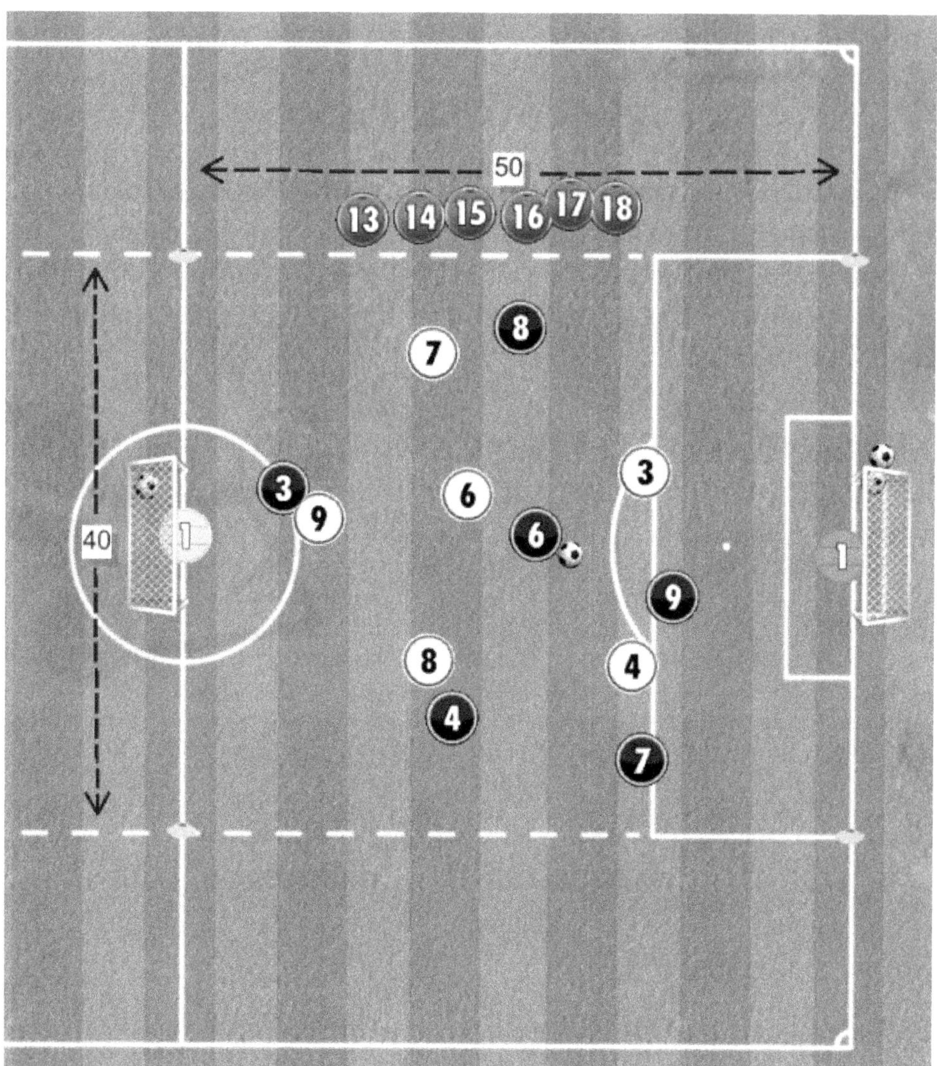

In play: Take note here, seeing as Black #6 has good possession, a midfielder (Black #7) has pushed on to support the attack and a full back (black #4) has also pushed further up the pitch.

(Image: Session 3 Drill 3 - B)

SESSION 4 - SUPPORTING THE FORWARD PASS

The more a team can get the ball forward and the more players a team can get forward, the better the chance of scoring. Plus, if they lose possession they can press the opposition high up the field and win it back as they have numbers up there. This session works on making good forward passes and getting support as the ball moves forward.

SESSION 4 DRILL 1:

RONDO

PURPOSE:

Win the ball and then help your teammates keep good possession.

SET UP:

- 8 to 20 Players. Adjust the size of the circles accordingly.
- 10 Cones or Discs
- Circular area
- 15 minutes

THE DRILL:

Half the players in one circle with the other half in another circle with a 30 yard gap between.

One player from each team stands in the middle of the opposition's circle in preparation to win the ball.

Once play starts teams pass the ball trying to keep it off the opposition player/s. As soon as the opposition player/s win the ball they sprint to their circle and tag a teammate who sprints to the other circle to do the same.

First team to get all their players to win possession and get back to their circle wins.

Punishment (20 push ups etc) for the losing team.

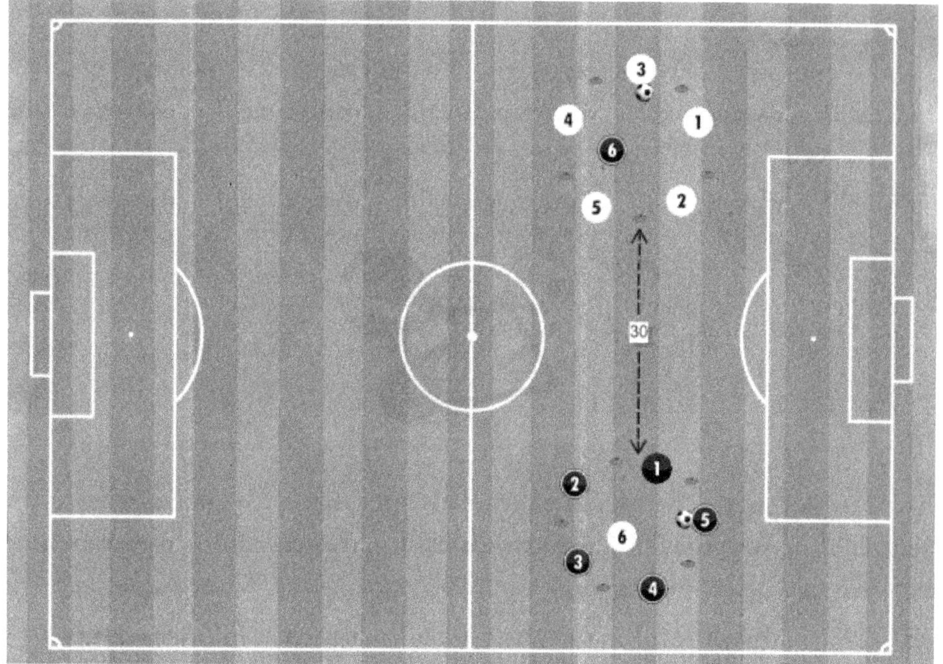

Starting shape: Example below is for 6v6. If numbers are greater, make the circle bigger and have 2 players looking to win possession.

(Image: Session 4 Drill 1 - A)

SESSION 4 DRILL 2:

FORWARD PASSING

PURPOSE:

This drill is aimed at improving players decision making so they don't force the forward pass when it's not on. But instead choose the right moment when they have good possession and the forward player is open to receive the pass.

SET UP:

- 9 Players (alternatively 6, 10 or 11)
- 4 Cones + 5 Discs
- 40x40 yard area
- 20 minutes

THE DRILL:

9 Players: 4 Blacks + 2 Greys v 3 Whites

10 and 11 players: Remove the goals and put a player there

6 Players: Make 2 quarters into a half. Remove one Black ,Grey and White player so it is 3+1v2

There are 4 squares with a Black player in each. 2 Grey players move between the squares to support the Black player in possession. The 3 White players can move between the squares looking to win possession but only 1 White player can be in any square at any given time.

The aim is for Blacks and Greys to combine, through short passes and good possession, to get the ball to the square that doesn't have a defender in it.

Once this happens the Black player can shoot into the small goal.

There must be 3 passes in a square before the ball can move to another..

If the Whites win possession, the whole square is open (no restrictions on where or how many players can be in a square at once). Whites keep it for as long as they can - the Greys are now on the Whites team making it 5v4 - and the 4 Black players have to win it back.

Once Blacks win back possession, players reset play restarts from any square.

KEY POINTS:

- The two Grey players must work hard to get into the square where the ball is. Once there they combine to have at least 3 passes before the ball can move to another square.

- All players must be switched on as the ball can come to them at any point. Especially the White defenders as one will need to move between squares to stop the attackers getting it to the spare Black player who can shoot.

- When Blacks lose possession it is vital that they try and win possession back straight away. This is because that is how it is done in a real game situation and they will be outnumbered so the best time to win back possession is in the first 3-5 seconds before the opposition get organised.

COACHES NOTES:

- Please be aware that this drill can seem very confusing for the players when they first do it. But it is well worth using and players get a lot out of it when it is in full swing. Explain it to them for a minute, then do a slow walk through.

- To sum it up for the players: The Blacks stay in their square. The 2 Greys move everywhere to support the Black player in possession. The 3 Whites move between squares trying to win possession but only 1 can be in a square at once.

- Swap the players over every couple of minutes as it is high intensity, especially for the 2 Grey players.

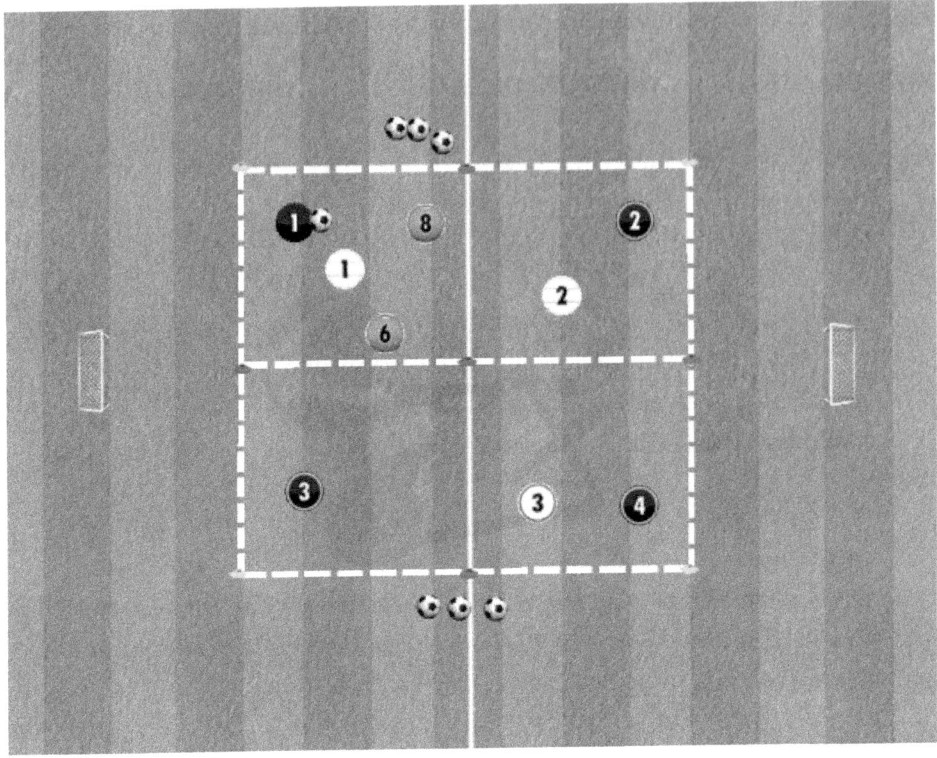

Starting shape: One Black in each of the squares. Here Black #1 has possession so the two Greys enter the square to support him and a White has entered to try and win the ball. The 3 players (2 Blacks & 1 Grey) must make 3 passes before the ball can go to another square.

If they can get it to Black #3 while there is no White defender he can shoot on goal.

(Image: Session 4 Drill 2 - A)

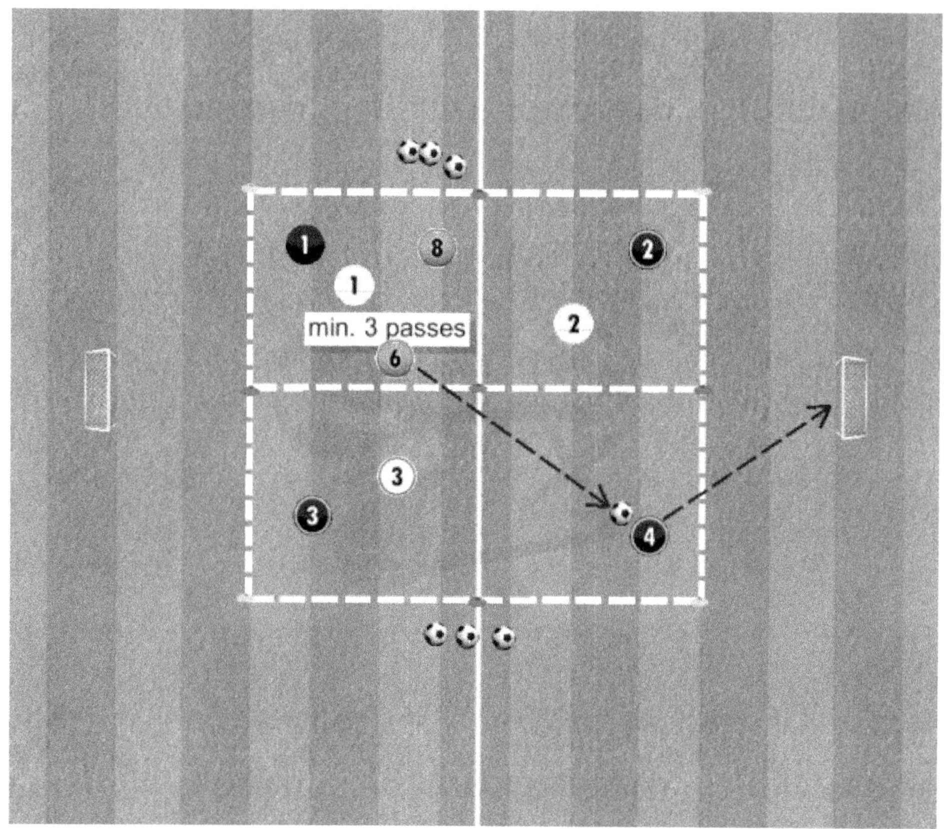

In play 1: Here the attackers have had at least three passes and have found an open attacker (Black #4) without a defender with him so he can shoot into the goal.

(Image: Session 4 Drill 2 - B)

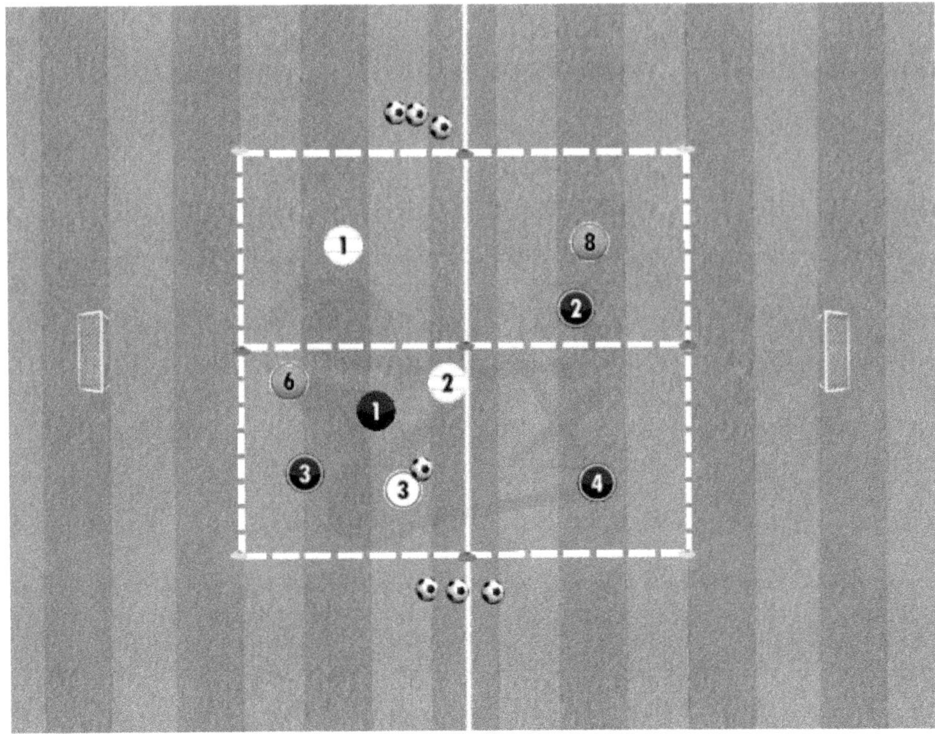

In play 2: Here, the White #3 defender has won possession. Play is now open with no restrictions on where you can go. Whites and Greys now play together with the Blacks trying to win back possession as soon as possible.

This teaches the players to work hard as soon as losing possession as this is the best time to win the ball back.

Once Black wins the ball back, players reset.

(Image: Session 4 Drill 2 - C)

SOME OF MY FAVOURITE PLAYERS (from my youth):

ROBERTO BAGGIO - I could watch him play all day long. So creative.

DIEGO MARADONNA - The same, what a genius. The best ever.

CHRIS WADDLE - One of the first players I took notice of growing up. Superb close control.

RYAN GIGGS - Gees! How'd you like to have him running at you one on one? Plus I think he was the last good crosser of the ball I can think of.

LOTHAR MATTHAUS - What a leader and a winner. Great engine and could score from miles out.

TWO OF MY FAVOURITE TEAM (from my youth):

AC MILAN & AJAX (of the late 80's/90's)

SESSION 4 DRILL 3:

LARGE GAME - SUPPORTING THE FORWARD PASS

PURPOSE:

To make players aware how important it is to push numbers forward when a forward pass has been made.

SET UP:

- 18 Players (Alternatively 16 to 22. Adjust the size of the area accordingly)

- 4 cones and 6 Discs

- 3/4 of a full pitch (alternatively half or full pitch depending on the amount of players)

- 2 Large goals (or 1 large goal and poles for the other one. Or if no Goalkeepers just use small goals)

- 20 minutes

THE DRILL:

2 teams of 9 players (including Goalkeepers). The pitch is marked into 3 even thirds.

Formations for each team should be as follows:

9 players: 3-3-2

10 players: 4-3-2

11 players: 4-3-3

A standard game but players must stay in their thirds until a forward pass is made. Once a pass has been made to the next third, one of the players from the team in possession must move forward into the next third to support their teammates. A goal cannot be scored unless a player from that team has moved forward into the furthest third.

KEY POINTS:

- Look to make a forward pass whenever a good opportunity presents itself (don't force it if it isn't there - keep possession until it does).

- Make sure a player is getting forward to support the forward pass.

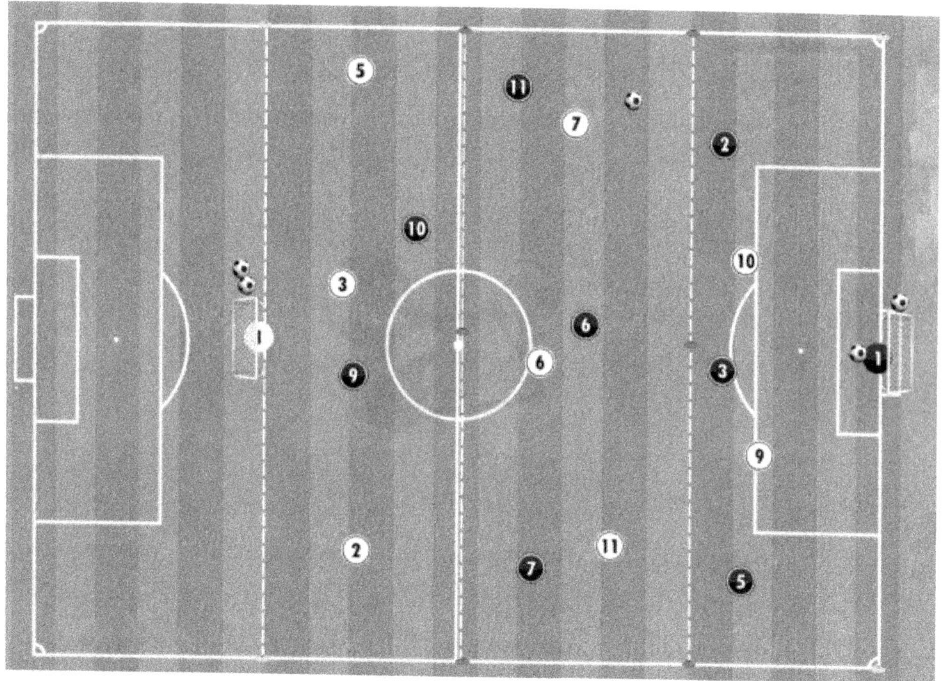

Starting shape: 3-3-2 formation for both teams. Play starts from the keepers. Players must stay in their third until a forward pass has been made to the middle third and then a player from that team can move into that third. Once a pass has been made from the middle third to the front third a player must again move forward into that third.

A goal can only be scored once that team has a player that has moved from the middle third to the front third.

(Image: Session 4 Drill 3- A)

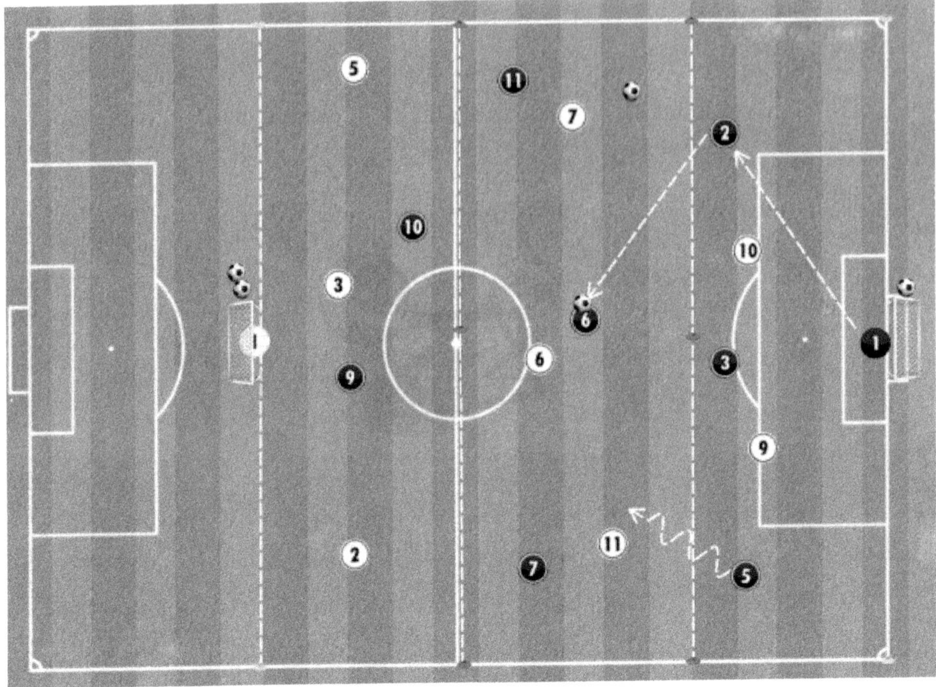

In play: In this image, the keeper has played it out to Black #2 who in turn plays it to Black #6 in the middle third. This is the trigger for any three of the Black defenders (#2,#3,#5) to move into the middle third to support the forward pass. In this instance it is Black #5.

(Image: Session 4 Drill 3 - B)

In play: The ball is then passed to Black #10 who can only shoot on goal once a supporting player from his team has made the run into the final third - in this case Black #7 makes the run. If a team scores they get to keep the ball and play restarts from their keeper.

(Image: Session 4 Drill 3- C)

That's all of the drills for this book. How to run the FIFA+ Warm Up and the Warm Down are after the "Tips on How to be a Better Coach".

It will take you and your players a couple of run throughs to work on what you are trying to achieve in each drill. But with practice will come speed and quality and your team will greatly improve, as will your coaching.

On the next few pages, there is some general advice on how to run a better session. It's things that I've found help me to be more organised, relaxed and productive when coaching, hopefully you will use a few of them.

Chris King website: www.chriskingsoccercoach.com[1]

- Training Sessions For Soccer Coaches Volume 1
- Attacking & Shooting Drills For Soccer Coaches
- Soccer Rondos - The Key To A Better Training Session
- Coaching Kids Soccer

1. http://www.chriskingsoccercoach.com

TIPS ON HOW TO BE A BETTER COACH

I'll admit I'm not the most organised person in the world. But when it comes to coaching a team or club you have no choice! If you're not an organised person by nature, learn how to be on the training track. It will save you a lot of time and you'll enjoy yourself more!

Here's the big one: Don't wait until 30 minutes before your session starts to plan what you are going to do!

I know life gets in the way, but simply spend a bit of time the night before or earlier that day/week to choose which session you're going to run

Use the drills in this book and the advice below and you'll be fine, it'll only take you 10 minutes to plan a session.

Then, on the day of the training, simply refresh yourself with it for 5 minutes before you arrive at training. (Once you get to training, if you're a head coach you will have other players and coaches asking you questions, so have a quick look at the session while you have time to yourself, even if it's in the car once you arrive at training).

You will find you will be a more relaxed and effective coach if you have spent time planning prior to arriving and this will show in your session.

Okay, with that out of the way here are some other tips for you...

Set your drills up prior to the session starting

If you have access to the ground prior to your training starting time, have as many of your drills set out as possible! I can't stress this enough. Step out your distances, put your cones down, have your bibs put down in the appropriate areas of your drill, bring out the small goals, have the balls spread around the drill. You get your players for approximately 90 minutes of good quality training, so don't waste 10-15 minutes of it setting up drills during a session while your players get cold and bored.

Have enough balls

If possible, have 10-15 balls (assuming you are training 12 to 14 players).Don't just have 3 balls which the players spend half their time chasing around. Do you think Andre Agassi won Grand Slams because he had one tennis ball and he retrieved it every time he miss hit it? No. His father bought a ball machine and fired hundreds and hundreds of tennis balls at him. Then they collected them when they needed a quick break.

So have as many soccer balls as possible on hand so the players get maximum value out of the drill. When the balls run out, get all the players to stop and collect them and go again. Or alternatively, get two of the juniors to stay behind and be ball boys/girls for the night and give them a can of Coke.

Players training gear in the one spot

If the players need a drink or they need to put on a top, you don't want them going miles away. Get them to put their drinks, spare boots, tops etc that they may need in the session close by in the one area so they are not running off for minutes at a time in all different directions.

Use flat discs on the field

Use a normal cone to mark the outside of an area, but if you need to mark out a square or line inside the main area, use flat discs so the players and balls don't hit them. They cost $5 for 10 from a sports store and will save time and frustration.

Keep all your gear separate from other coaches

Sorry to sound selfish, but if at all possible, keep a ball bag with all your balls and another bag with bibs, cones and discs either at your place or at the club but don't let other teams use it. I know this may not be possible due to lack of funds at a lot of clubs, but if at all possible take most of your gear with you after each session. If this isn't possible, even if you just buy some bibs and cones and keep those separate so you're not running around prior to training wondering where they've all disappeared to. You will be glad come next training session that you have all your gear with you and not here, there and everywhere.

And lastly...

Don't over explain a drill

Don't spend 10 minutes going through every detail with the players - most of them will learn by doing.

Simply give a quick 1 to 2 minute explanation of the drill, the rules and what you want them to get out of it and then say "Right we're live!" and start playing.

Once it's been going for a couple of minutes, then you can pause the drill and reconfirm anything the players are struggling to grasp. This has also given you time to make sure that you've got the drill running as you hoped (if you have to adjust the size of the areas or change players positions etc you can do it now).

Sometimes the longer you explain things at the start, the more confused players become and the more questions they ask. So initially just have a quick explanation and then start the drill. Too easy!

WARM UP: FIFA 11+ OFFICIAL WARM UP

For the last three seasons we have implemented the FIFA 11+ warm up at our club and we have benefited from it. After two weeks of showing the players what to do they were running most of the warm up by themselves. The coaches literally set up the cones and then when it was time to start the warm up, simply said "Right, get in your pairs and away you go please".

The FIFA 11+ warm up has been shown to reduce major injuries by 50% in recreational/sub-elite football. It consists of three parts with a total of 15 exercises performed in order. It should be performed at the start of every training session.

You should use it as the warm up prior to matches as well but only the running exercises (parts 1 and 3), don't do the core and leg strengthening.

I have inserted an image in the next page but if you are reading this on a device with a small screen you may struggle, so simply Google "FIFA 11+" or I would suggest going to the following site so you can see it in practice:

http://www.f-marc.com/exercises/ and

http://www.f-marc.com/home-3/ (this link gives you an overview of it and explains why it is important).

The FIFA 11+ program is broken down into 3 parts:

1. **Slow-speed running exercises coupled with active and partner stretching (8 minutes)**

1. **Core and leg strength exercises, along with balance, plyometrics, and agility exercises (12 minutes)**

1. **Moderate/high speed running exercises integrated with cutting and pivoting movements (2 minutes).**

Setting it up: There are six pairs of parallel cones, approximately 5-6m apart. Two players start at the same time from the first pair of cones, jog along the inside of the cones and do the various exercises on the way at each set of cones. After the last cone, they turn and run back along the outside. On the way back, speed can be increased progressively as players warm up.

The FIFA 11+ is well worth implementing. Most of it can be done in a fairly small area and the players look and feel more professional and therefore treat the rest of the session in a more professional manner.

On the following page is a breakdown of the exercises that are performed in the first part. I would still suggest going to http://www.f-marc.com/exercises/ and http://www.f-marc.com/home-3/ if you are unfamiliar with it as each exercise is shown in a video and explained.

The warm down after a training session or a game should be slow jogging and then walking with intermittent static stretches for approximately 10 minutes.

1. Straight Ahead: Jog straight to the last cone. Run slightly more quickly on the way back. Do the exercise 2x.

2. Running Hip Out: Jog to the first cone. Stop and lift your knee forwards. Rotate your knee to the side and put your foot down. Jog to the cone and do the exercise on the other leg. When you have finished the course, jog back. Do the exercise 2x.

3. Running Hip In: Jog to the first cone. Stop and lift your knee to the side. Rotate your knee forwards and put your foot down. Jog to the next cone and do the exercise on the other leg. When you have finished the course, jog back. Do the exercise 2x.

4. Circling Partner: Jog forwards to the first cone. Shuffle sideways at a 90 degree angle towards our partner, shuffle an entire circle around one another (without changing the direction you are looking in) and back to the first cone. Jog to the next cone and repeat the exercise. When you have finished the course, jog back. Do the exercise 2x.

5. Jumping with Shoulder Contact: Jog to the first cone. Shuffle sideways at a 90 degree angle towards your partner. In the middle, jump sideways towards each other to make shoulder-to-shoulder contact. Shuffle back to the first cone. Then jog to the next cone and repeat the exercise. When you have finished the course, jog back. Do the exercise 2x.

6. Quick Forwards and Backwards Sprints: Run quickly to the second cone then run backwards quickly to the first cone, keeping your hips and knees slightly bent. Repeat, running two cones forwards and one cone backwards. When you have finished the course, jog back. Do the exercise 2x.

You should try not to have long gaps between activities. When your warm up is complete, have a quick break for a drink, explain the next drill and then start.

FIFA 11+
RUNNING EXERCISES · 8 MINUTES
STRAIGHT AHEAD
HIP OUT
HIP IN
CIRCLING PARTNER
SHOULDER CONTACT
QUICK FORWARDS & BACKWARDS
STRENGTH · PLYOMETRICS · BALANCE · 10 MINUTES
STATIC
ALTERNATE LEGS
ONE LEG LIFT AND HOLD
STATIC
RAISE & LOWER HIP
WITH LEG LIFT
BEGINNER
INTERMEDIATE
ADVANCED
HOLD THE BALL
THROWING BALL WITH PARTNER
TEST YOUR PARTNER
WITH TOE RAISE
WALKING LUNGES
ONE-LEG SQUATS
VERTICAL JUMPS
LATERAL JUMPS
BOX JUMPS
RUNNING EXERCISES · 2 MINUTES
ACROSS THE PITCH
BOUNDING
PLANT & CUT
F-MARC
FIFA
FIFA

THANK YOU!

Thank you for the support, I hope you got some valuable information from the sessions . Please spend one minute giving the book a rating to help others find my book.

Thanks again and all the best with your coaching!

Chris King

'Til next time, thanks again and all the best with your coaching.

And if you need full sessions, get hold of my other books which have 4 full sessions in each book. Just search for:

"Chris King Soccer Coach".

Online Kids Coaching Course on Udemy.com:

https://www.udemy.com/course/

howtocoachkidssoccer/?referralCode=CCFEDDB18FE0AAF8F1CC

VIEW OTHER SOCCER COACHING BOOKS BY CHRIS KING

Training Sessions For Soccer Coaches Volume 1

Training Sessions For Soccer Coaches Volume 2

Training Sessions For Soccer Coaches Volume 3

Attacking & Shooting Drills For Soccer Coaches

Soccer Rondos Volume 1

Soccer Rondos Volume 2

Coaching Kids Soccer - Volume 1

Coaching Kids Soccer - Volume 2

Coaching Kids Soccer - Volume 3

The Ultimate Soccer Coaching Bundle Volume 1

TRAINING SESSIONS FOR
SOCCER
COACHES
VOLUME 1
Coaching Books For Amateur Soccer Coaches
CHRIS KING

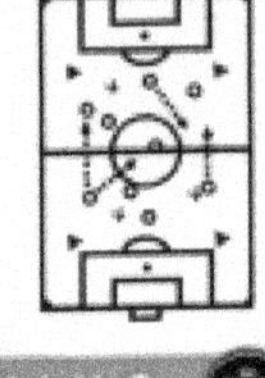

TRAINING SESSIONS FOR
SOCCER
COACHES
VOLUME 2
Coaching Books For Amateur Soccer Coaches
CHRIS KING

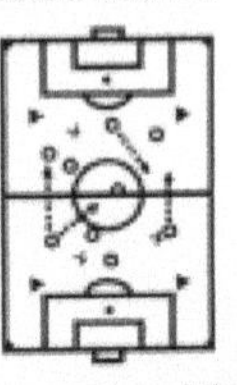

TRAINING SESSIONS FOR
SOCCER
COACHES
VOLUME 3
Coaching Books For Amateur Soccer Coaches
CHRIS KING
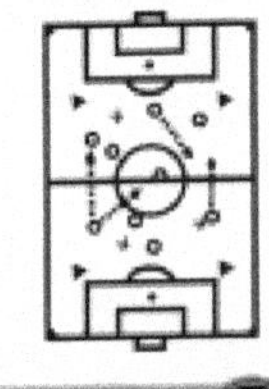

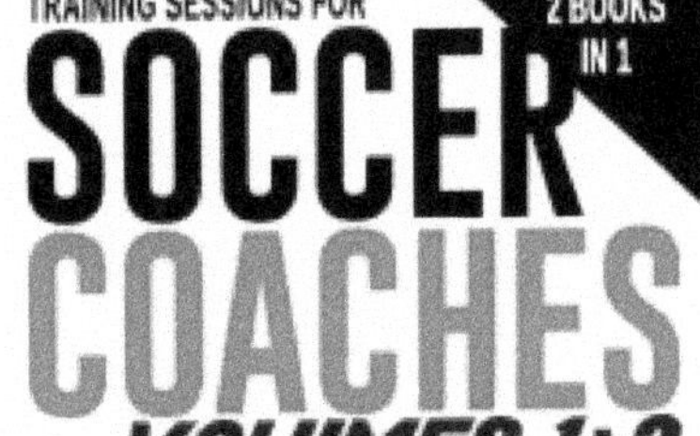
TRAINING SESSIONS FOR
SOCCER
2 BOOKS IN 1
COACHES
VOLUMES 1+2
Coaching Books For Amateur Soccer Coaches
CHRIS KING

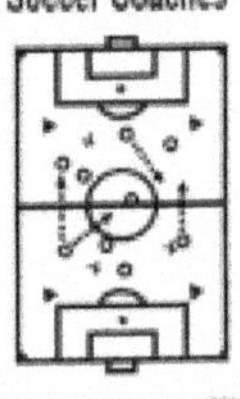

TRAINING SESSIONS FOR
SOCCER
COACHES
3 BOOKS IN 1!
VOLUMES 1,2,3
Coaching Books For Amateur Soccer Coaches
CHRIS KING
ATTACKING & SHOOTING DRILLS FOR
SOCCER
COACHES
VOLUME 1
Coaching Books For Amateur Soccer Coaches
CHRIS KING

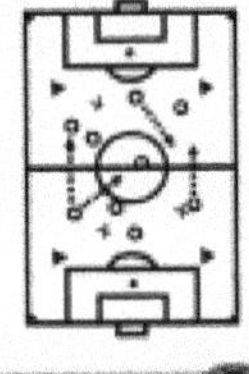
SOCCER
RONDOS
VOLUME 1
Coaching Books For Amateur Soccer Coaches
CHRIS KING

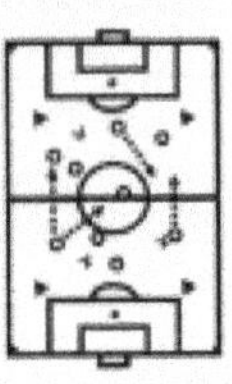

SOCCER
RONDOS
VOLUME 2
Coaching Books For Amateur Soccer Coaches
CHRIS KING

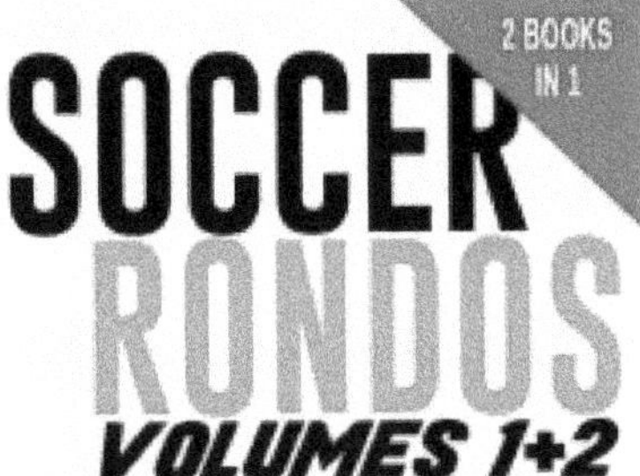

2 BOOKS
IN 1
SOCCER
RONDOS
VOLUMES 1+2
Coaching Books For Amateur Soccer Coaches
CHRIS KING

COACHING KIDS SOCCER
AGES 5 TO 10
VOLUME 1
This book is for first time coaches, volunteers, parents and anyone wanting to coach!
Set up simple, fun and effective drills and organise a training session in 5 minutes!
CHRIS KING
COACHING KIDS SOCCER
AGES 5 TO 10
VOLUME 2
This book is for first time coaches, grassroots coaches, volunteers and parents!
Set up simple soccer drills that teach kids skills while having fun!
CHRIS KING
COACHING KIDS SOCCER
AGES 5 TO 10
VOLUME 3
This book is for first time coaches, volunteers & any would be coach
Set up simple, fun and effective drills & organise a practice session in 5 minutes!
CHRIS KING
2 BOOKS IN 1
COACHING KIDS SOCCER
VOLUMES 1-2
This book is for first time coaches, volunteers & any would be coach
Set up simple fun and effective drills & organise a practice session in 5 minutes!
CHRIS KING

Or sign up for a free soccer eBook at www.chriskingsoccercoach.com[1]

1. http://www.chriskingsoccercoach.com

WORD INDEX

Buy-In - Meaning that the players or other coaches can see the benefits and therefore should perform better, enjoy it more and attend more sessions.

FIFI 11+ Warm Up - The accepted FIFA warm up that is performed prior to any drills. Benefits of using this are that it has been shown to reduce injury.

Head Checks - Looking over your shoulder and around the pitch so you know who is around you and where you will pass the ball when you receive it. Very important for a midfielder.

Overload Player - The player in a drill who plays on the team in possession and creates an extra player over the opposition. They usually wear a different colour bib. For example if Blue are playing Red, the overload player would wear Yellow so both teams know.

Passing Lanes - These are simply the lines that a player would look to pass to another player. So to block the pass you should get in between the two players in the passing lane. It can be forward, sideways, backwards - wherever the opposition's team mate is, this is where a player should be.

Pressing Triggers - A trigger is something that happens on the pitch that makes the players react and perform a task. In this case the trigger is a sign for the players to press the opposition (get close and try and win the ball off the ball carrier). Triggers for a press would be: a bad or slow pass; the opposition player having bad body shape; playing backwards etc. If you see one of these, it's a trigger to press and the team all press at once.

Progression - When you want to take the drill into a different or harder phase (to stretch the players). You should start with the original drill and move onto the progression once players are comfortable with the initial drill.

Rondo - A small drill that is used at the start of training (straight after the warm up) to get everyone switched on and get lots of touches on the ball. There are many different ones, they should be enjoyable with intensity.

Third Line Passing - The penetrative pass between two defenders. This is important as if this pass is made two defensive players are taken out of the game. First line is sideways and the second line is sideways but forward.

Don't miss out!

Visit the website below and you can sign up to receive emails whenever Chris King publishes a new book. There's no charge and no obligation.

https://books2read.com/r/B-A-QGPU-RSONC

BOOKS 2 READ

Connecting independent readers to independent writers.

Also by Chris King

Coaching Kids Soccer

Coaching Kids Soccer - Ages 5 to 10 - Volume 1

Coaching Kids Soccer - Ages 5 to 10 - Volume 2

Coaching Kids Soccer - Ages 5 to 10 - Volume 3

Coaching Kids Soccer - Ages 5 to 10 - Volumes 1,2,3

Coaching Kids Soccer - Volumes 1 & 2

Coaching Soccer

Training Sessions For Soccer Coaches - Volume 1

Training Sessions For Soccer Coaches

Training Sessions For Soccer Coaches Volume 2

Training Sessions For Soccer Coaches Volume 3

The Ultimate Soccer Coaching Bundle (5 books in 1) Volume 1

Training Sessions For Soccer Coaches Volumes 1-2-3

www.ingramcontent.com/pod-product-compliance
Ingram Content Group UK Ltd.
Pitfield, Milton Keynes, MK11 3LW, UK
UKHW021925190726
13853UKWH00002B/846

9 798215 267516